Great Americans

Anne Hutchinson

Barbara Kiely Miller

Reading consultant: Susan Nations, M.Ed., author/literacy coach/
consultant in literacy development

WEEKLY READER®
PUBLISHING

Please visit our web site at: www.garethstevens.com
For a free color catalog describing our list of high-quality books,
call 1-800-542-2595 (USA) or 1-800-387-3178 (Canada).

Library of Congress Cataloging-in-Publication Data

Kiely Miller, Barbara.
    Anne Hutchinson / by Barbara Kiely Miller.
        p. cm. — (Great Americans)
    Includes bibliographical references and index.
    ISBN-13: 978-0-8368-8317-6 (lib. bdg.)
    ISBN-13: 978-0-8368-8324-4 (softcover)
    ISBN-10: 0-8368-8317-9 (lib. bdg.)
    ISBN-10: 0-8368-8324-1 (softcover)
    1. Hutchinson, Anne Marbury, 1591-1643—Juvenile literature.
2. Puritans—Massachusetts—Biography—Juvenile literature.
3. Puritan women—Massachusetts—Biography—Juvenile literature.
4. Massachusetts—History—Colonial period, ca. 1600-1775—Juvenile
literature. I. Title.
F67.H92K54   2008
973.2'2092—dc22   2007016894

This edition first published in 2008 by
Weekly Reader® Books
An imprint of Gareth Stevens Publishing
1 Reader's Digest Road
Pleasantville, NY 10570-7000 USA

Copyright © 2008 by Gareth Stevens, Inc.

Managing editor: Valerie J. Weber
Art direction: Tammy West
Cover design and page layout: Charlie Dahl
Picture research: Sabrina Crewe
Production: Jessica Yanke

Picture credits: Cover, title page © Bettmann/Corbis; pp. 5, 12, 16, 19 The Granger
Collection, New York; p. 6 David Jones Photography; pp. 7, 8, Mary Evans Picture Library;
pp. 9, 13, 17, 18 © North Wind Picture Archives; p. 11 Charlie Dahl/© Gareth Stevens, Inc.;
p. 14 © Corbis; p. 21 © Kevin Fleming/Corbis.

Printed in the United States of America

1 2 3 4 5 6 7 8 9 11 10 09 08 07

Table of Contents

Chapter 1: An Independent Thinker 4

Chapter 2: Looking for Freedom in America . 10

Chapter 3: A Woman on Trial 15

Chapter 4: A Pioneer for Freedom 20

Glossary 22

For More Information 23

Index 24

Cover and title page: Anne Hutchinson fought for religious freedom in colonial America during the 1600s.

Chapter 1

An Independent Thinker

Anne Hutchinson was excited as she spoke to the
women and men in her home. They had prayed and
talked about their **minister's sermon**, or lesson. Anne
loved to share her ideas about religion. She did not
always agree, however, with what her church's
ministers taught.

Hutchinson lived in the early 1600s, when people were not always free to say what they thought. They could not **worship** the way they wanted. Anne Hutchinson fought for these freedoms. Although she did not live to see it, these freedoms would become part of every American's life.

Thanks to Anne Hutchinson, other early settlers in America were free to worship the way they wanted.

Anne was born in 1591 in England. Her father, Francis Marbury, was a minister. He often **preached**, or talked, about what he thought was wrong with the Church of England. The church's leaders silenced Francis. They said he had to stop being a minister.

Anne's father preached at St. Wilfrid's Church in Alford, England. Built in 1350, the church is still used today.

Anne Marbury was taught at home, learning to read from her father's sermons and plays. She studied the Bible and her father's books about religion. When Francis and his friends discussed religion and government, Anne listened closely. She learned to form her own ideas and to say what she thought.

This painting shows the kind of clothing that Anne Hutchinson probably wore.

This picture from the 1600s shows two tailors making clothes. William Hutchinson made clothing, too.

When she was twenty-one years old, Anne married William Hutchinson. He was a merchant, selling clothes for men. Like her mother, Anne became a **midwife**, helping women give birth. Together, William and Anne had fifteen children of their own!

Anne still had time for church, however. She liked the sermons of **Puritan** minister John Cotton. The Puritans wanted to change the Church of England. They wanted simpler churches and to choose their own ministers. Puritans were punished for their beliefs. In 1633, John Cotton left England and sailed to North America.

© North Wind Picture Archives

John Cotton was a minister at a church in Boston, England. His preaching reminded Anne Hutchinson of her father's sermons.

Chapter 2

Looking for Freedom in America

During the 1600s, many people in Great Britain wanted religious freedom. They founded new colonies in North America. Anne Hutchinson wanted to be free to worship and talk about her beliefs, too. In 1634, she and her family moved to the Massachusetts Bay Colony. They settled in Boston, where Cotton now lived.

Being a midwife helped Anne make friends easily with other women. She invited her friends to prayer meetings in her home. Each week, they talked about Cotton's sermon. Then they would pray and study the Bible. Anne felt free to tell the women her ideas about religion.

This map shows the cities in present-day North America where the Hutchinson family lived after leaving England.

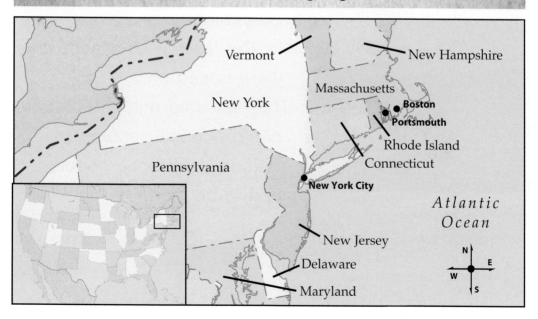

Anne spoke to large groups in her home. Not everyone liked her ideas.

Soon men came to Anne's meetings, too. They had heard she was smart and a great speaker. Anne started sharing beliefs that were different than those taught by the Puritan ministers. Some people thought Anne was preaching.

The laws in Massachusetts were based on the Bible. The law said only the church could choose people to preach, and those people had to be men.

The more Anne talked, the more trouble she got into. She argued that people did not need ministers or the Bible. She said anyone could talk directly to God. Puritan ministers said people needed the Bible to worship God. They also claimed that only they knew what the Bible meant.

© North Wind Picture Archives

A Puritan minister is shown preaching from the Bible in a Boston church.

SʳᵅHENRY VANE.

While he was governor, Henry Vane supported Hutchinson and came to her meetings.

Some of the men at Anne's meetings were government leaders. They supported her right to say what she thought. Other people said her ideas were wrong. They also said men and women should not be meeting together in private.

In 1637, John Winthrop became governor. Like many others, he thought women should always obey men and should not be teaching religion.

Chapter 3

A Woman on Trial

Anne Hutchinson began saying that the ministers' teachings were wrong. Church leaders and government leaders worried that people would no longer listen to them. Governor Winthrop said Anne was trying to bring down the government. He had her arrested!

At her **trial**, Anne had no one to help her. Governor Winthrop led forty-nine men in questioning Anne about her religious beliefs. She knew the Bible as well as they did, however. She used the Bible to say why she was right.

John Winthrop was the first governor of Massachusetts Bay Colony. A powerful man, he served as governor twelve times.

Anne argued that many Puritans in England had meetings in their homes to discuss religion. She stated that God spoke to her directly and only God could judge her. The men said Anne was guilty of speaking against the government, however.

The Puritan leaders also wanted Anne to say that her ideas were wrong. When she refused, they said she could no longer belong to the church.

© North Wind Picture Archives

Anne Hutchinson stood alone at her trial and fought for her beliefs.

When people were forced out of Massachusetts, they had to leave their belongings and search for a new home in another colony.

In 1638, the government forced Anne and her family to leave Massachusetts. They moved to Aquidneck Island. Anne helped start the settlement of Portsmouth, which later became part of Rhode Island. Rhode Island became the first colony to say that the government could not tell people how to worship.

William Hutchinson died in 1642. Anne moved to what became New York City with her six youngest children. On August 20, 1643, a group of Native Americans attacked settlers in the area. Anne and five of her children were killed.

The governor of New York was not friendly to the Native Americans who lived there. The Indians became angry and killed several people, including Anne and her family.

Chapter 4

A Pioneer for Freedom

The story of Anne Hutchinson's trial spread throughout America's colonies. People's longing for religious freedom grew. About 150 years after Anne's death, this need was finally met. In 1791, the United States approved the Bill of Rights. This document said the government could not set up any religion and that people were free to worship the way they wanted.

Anne's arguments for her prayer meetings influenced laws, too. The Bill of Rights also says people are free to meet in groups and are free to say what they want. Anne Hutchinson is most remembered, however, as a pioneer of religious freedom.

A statue honors Anne Hutchinson in front of the Massachusetts State House in Boston. Hutchinson still stands for religious freedom in the United States.

Glossary

Bill of Rights — a paper that says what people in a country can do

colonies — places that are controlled by a government in another country

governor — a person who is chosen to govern a colony or territory

influenced — changed or had an effect on something or someone

merchant — someone who sells goods

midwife — a woman who helps others give birth

minister — a religious leader of a church

preached — gave a sermon or talk about a religious subject, usually in a church

Puritan — a member of the Church of England who wanted to change its organization and ceremonies

sermon — a speech that explains religious beliefs or morals

trial — a meeting in court to decide whether someone did something against the law

worship — to honor and love a divine being such as a god or goddess or to take part in a religious service

For More Information

Books

Anne Hutchinson. American Lives (series). Elizabeth Raum (Heinemann Library)

Anne Hutchinson. Discover the Life of a Colonial American (series). Kieran Walsh (Rourke Publishing)

M Is for Mayflower: A Massachusetts Alphabet. Discover America by State (series). Margot Theis Raven (Sleeping Bear Press)

Web Sites

Harcourt Multimedia Biographies — Anne Hutchinson
www.harcourtschool.com/activity/biographies/hutchinson
Read another story about Anne Hutchinson.

Stand up for Your Rights: The Trial of Anne Hutchinson
pbskids.org/wayback/civilrights/features_hutchison.html
Read more about Anne Hutchinson's fight for religious freedom.

Index

Bible, the 7, 11, 12, 13, 16
Bill of Rights 20, 21
books 7
Boston 10, 13, 21

churches 4, 6, 9, 12, 13, 15, 17
clothing 7, 8
colonies 10, 18, 20
Cotton, John 9, 10, 11

England 6, 9, 10, 11, 17

families 6, 7, 8, 19

freedoms 5, 10, 20, 21

governments 7, 14, 15, 17, 18, 20
governors 14, 16, 19

Massachusetts Bay Colony 10, 12, 16, 18
meetings 11, 12, 14, 17, 21
midwives 8, 11
ministers 4, 6, 9, 12, 13, 15

praying 7, 11, 21
preaching 6, 9, 12, 13
Puritans 9, 12, 13, 17

Rhode Island 18

sermons 4, 7, 9, 11
settlers 5, 19

trials 16, 17, 20

Winthrop, John 14, 15, 16
worshipping 5, 10, 13, 18, 20

About the Author

Barbara Kiely Miller is an editor and writer of educational books for children. She has a degree in creative writing from the University of Wisconsin–Milwaukee. Barbara lives in Shorewood, Wisconsin, with her husband and their two cats Ruby and Sophie. When she is not writing or reading books, Barbara enjoys photography, bicycling, and gardening.